Pussy Liberty

A One Act Play

by Valerie Isaiah Sadoh

The Bread & Roses Theatre
68 Clapham Manor Street
London SW4 6DZ
www.breadandrosestheatre.co.uk

© Valerie Isaiah Sadoh.

First published by The Bread & Roses Theatre in 2018.

Valerie Isaiah Sadoh has asserted her right to be identified as the author of this work. All rights reserved. Requests to reproduce the text in whole or in part should be addressed to the publisher.

Cover illustration: Lizzie Knott
Design/Formatting: Tessa Hart

ISBN 978-1-912504-02-2

Amateur and Professional Performing Rights

No performance of any kind of this play may be given unless a licence has been obtained, including excerpts and readings. Application should be made before rehearsals begin. Publication of these plays does not indicate availability for performance. This applies to all mediums and all languages.

To enquire about availability for performing rights and the necessary steps to undertake to obtain a licence, please contact info@breadandrosestheatre.co.uk in the first instance.

Valerie Isaiah Sadoh
Valerie Isaiah Sadoh trained at Identity School of Acting, the UK's award-winning part-time drama school. After initially working as an actress she lamented the lack of interesting stories and characters for women. Using her English Literature and Physical Theatre skills, she took the power into her own hands and began to write for her local communities, co-writing youth theatre production 'LOUD' which was taken to Rwanda in 2015 and short film 'Condemned in the City' about domestic abuse in a relationship.

Pussy Liberty by Valerie Isaiah Sadoh

Pussy Liberty was first performed at The Bread & Roses Theatre from 15th to 19th August 2017, after the producing company ***She's Diverse*** won The Bread & Roses Emerging Companies Award 2017.

It was presented with the following cast and creatives:

CAST

Blaire- Marie Myrie

Halle- Annabelle Broad

George- Kyran Mitchell-Nanton

Nurse- Kellie McCord

Narrator- Julia Xavier Stier

CREATIVES

Director- Diana Mumbi

Lighting/Sound Operator- Katherine Young

Producer- She's Diverse Full Sail Productions

Production Graphics- Jerome Ghartey

Photographer- Amanda Easmon

Illustrator- Lizzie Knott

"Thank you to The Old Diorama Arts Centre, to Dorothy Sadoh, and all those who donated along the way, we wouldn't have come this far without you all."
- Valerie Isaiah Sadoh with the cast & crew

Characters

Blaire – (25) Black British Female.

Halle- (25) Caucasian British Female.

George- (27) Black British Male

Nurse – (44) Local GUM clinic NHS worker

Narrator present throughout play

Setting

East London- Bethnal Green

Time

21st Century (Age of The Millennials)

Key

/- more than one person speaks at the same time

//- character is interrupted

Italics- stage directions

SCENE ONE

Spotlight on Blaire as she struggles to get a perched no contact position to the toilet in her local Family Planning Clinic.

Narrator
Day One of Rehabilitation, questioning the very reason you entertained the fact that you were sick anyway

Blaire
I'm not the only one to make up some elaborate story about having a long-term boyfriend and how things are going amazingly well. Just to avoid the side eye the nurse gives you when you're back for the third time this month with a different partner. Alfred my ex, clingy as anything! I mean come on, still get lifts to work from his mum. Felt somewhat perverted so I moved on to Jordan and rightfully so. The guy carried dental floss around. Right? Adult-ing at its best.
So what was wrong with him? High maintenance as Fack
Like please I nearly got my head cut off for eating in bed. How are you watching Scandal without a few Custard Creams?

Blaire looks down at the pot she is urinating in and then addresses the audience

Is that enough piss because they never tell you?

Stranger knocks on cubical door impatiently

Sorry! I'll be out in a sec

Nurse
You're very brave for taking this step

Blaire
My mum used to say I was quite the Viking

Blaire grunts and mimics a Viking

Nurse
Right, it's very hard sometimes for us to re live things that have hurt us

Blaire
I mean it's a Tuesday morning and I quite fancied the time off work

Nurse stares at Blaire unsure of the joke

Blaire
I did see the poster that said if you have an unhealthy relationship with sex gives a call. I didn't give a call straight away I did this online test I found on Google. Nimpho or not.com and I got 86% result rate.

86%, passed my driving test on 58% so it turns out I'm super qualified to be a sex addict, who would have thought?

Nurse
I like you. But I'm afraid it doesn't work like that.
If you don't mind me asking, when did you lose your virginity?

Narrator
Faces begin to flash before my eyes and my heart begins to beat and I remember what it's like to be free briefly before I'm captured and encaged. I have this reoccurring dream

Blaire
When?

Nurse
Ok, lets start with your family. Do you have siblings?

SCENE TWO

A beat. Nurse exits stage and Blaire is left on stage, changing from her uncomfortable and closed stance, to relaxed and sprawled out position. She is now home in her flat.

Blaire
How the hell can anyone get some peace and quiet with that in the bloody background?
Halle
Well if you'd wash your clothes you'd know that this is essential

Blaire
You know what else is essential? Relaxation time

Halle
You work two days a week

Blaire
I'm a creative

Halle/Blaire
Building an empire and a brand

Halle
Yeah, you've mentioned that once or twice

Blaire
Who's stuff is that anyway?

Halle
Just a few of George's shirts

Blaire
Why are you hiding it? Let me see

Blaire laughs and struggles to get a clear view of what Halle is doing

Blaire
A few? Fucking hell this is like the Roman Empire of laundry piles

Halle
His washing machine broke, plus he doesn't know how to get his collars sharp with out too much starch

Blaire
Sorry I couldn't hear you over Jane Anger rolling in her grave

Halle
Shut up, this is why I didn't want to tell you

Blaire
But I'm your best friend. I just think you're enabling him

Halle
I'm helping my man out. Calm down

Blaire
(Coughs) Male sympathiser

Halle
Why'd you hate men so much?

Blaire
I don't I just see them for what they are

Halle/ Blaire
Human beings?/Dog Shite

They both break into a little chuckle

Halle
Alright, I'm off. Leave these where they are okay.

SCENE THREE

Halle exits. Blaire turns up some Britney Spears and begins to dance around freely. Suddenly interrupted by George bursting in

George
Crap! Didn't realise you were in

Blaire
Surprised you didn't pay for the delivery service

George
(reluctantly laughs)
I come in peace, just wanted to be in and out

Blaire
Oh I *know* you're intentions

George
Ok, well if you don't mind you're blocking the way

Blaire
Me or women in general?

George
George notices the music playing in the background.
What dribble is this?

Blaire
Throwbacks songs

George
Sounds like a crap Britney Spears song

Blaire
There are no crap Britney Spears songs

George
You sure mate?

Blaire
Sure as can be. Mate.

George
Doesn't she go against your religion about women?

Blaire
She is the epitome of girl power, legacy, vulnerability and strength

George
Born to make you happy, My loneliness is killing me…

Blaire
Wow word for word, after all these years

George
I'm making a point

Blaire
I think you made my point!

George
You can't want a women's uprising and then praise the Britney Spears' of the world, it's a contradiction

Blaire
It's a contradiction because men like you are too simple minded to understand that women have layers

George
Layers of bullshit

Long Pause

Narrator
Faces begin to flash before my eyes and my heart begins to beat and I remember what it's like to be free briefly before I'm captured and encaged. I have this reoccurring dream

Doorbell rings frantically and both Blaire and George are startled out of their staring match. Halle then bursts through the door

Halle
Argh! I left my purse, got all the way to the station and started running around like a headless chicken. Oh hey babe

Blaire
On a scale of 1-10 how great are Britney Spears songs?

Halle
Pretty great

Blaire
I said a scale but okay, you see George. Classics

George
But are the content of the songs empowering in anyway?

Halle begins to ponder

George
Exactly

Blaire
Grow some balls

Halle
Who me?

Blaire
No the other male sympathiser

George
Where's my washing?

Halle/Blaire
Where it always is!

SCENE FOUR

Blackout then spotlight on Narrator. Narrator seems zombie like both in body language and speech

Narrator
Day Five of Rehabilitation, who's idea was it to heal? Mine or society? After all it wasn't my fault.

Blaire
True or False? I once squashed my pet hamster when I was seven.

Nurse
Last one and False

Blaire
Fine last one. You were right anyway. Being squashed is a really bad way to go

Nurse
Can we get back to it?

Blaire
Yeah go on

Nurse
You were telling me about your first boyfriend

Blaire
Was I?
He was tall for a year ten, had dark brown eyes and slits in his eyebrows. Back when that was a thing

Nurse
Not necessarily his looks

Blaire
I was in year seven

Nurse
Year seven, so eleven or twelve years old?

Blaire seems unnerved by the nurse dissecting her age

Narrator
Faces begin to flash before my eyes and my heart begins to beat and I remember what it's like to be free briefly before I'm captured and encaged. I have this reoccurring dream

Nurse
Was that relationship sexual?

Blaire
I was twelve

Nurse
I see

SCENE FIVE

Halle
I just don't think you're dating the right people

Blaire
No you don't say

Halle
You sure you don't want to double date with George and I. He said Alex was pretty awesome

Blaire
Yeah sure, let me wax my legs. Why didn't you say he was 'pretty awesome' before?

Halle
A simple no would have sufficed

Blaire
Would it? Something tells me you would have carried on begging

Halle
I'm going to be late

Blaire
Have fun don't let a spinster like me hold you up

Halle exits. Blaire inhales and exhales in a mini movement piece of frustration

Blaire
What haven't I watched on Netflix, yes Pretty Woman!

Blaire watches the audience as if it's the TV and mouths the words of Pretty Woman

Blaire
Its just very few people surprise me,
Well you're lucky people normally shock the hell out of me

I want the fairy tale

In case I forget to tell you later, I had a really good time tonight

Blaire begins to tear up and show her vulnerable side. Then the sound of keys interrupt her moment. Halle and George walk in

Halle
You could have told me George

George
You look fine

Blaire
Every girl's dream

George
Don't make this worse

Halle
I wore converses. The restaurant had marble falls and I wore converses

Blaire
Who gives a fuck

Halle
I do. I'm going to change

George looks at Blaire on the couch

George
No date?

Blaire
On a school night, never

George
Look if you need some dating advice I got you

Blaire
I'd rather die alone

George
I'm just saying

Blaire
I'm perfectly happy

George
I would be too, on a Thursday night surrounded by ice cream and cookies yum

Blaire
Look I'm very aware of what you're doing. Listen my idea of happiness isn't walking down the aisle in white

George
Its not?

Blaire
No, it's not

George
I'm sorry maybe it's the dream of being picked up from a long night shift by a rich man who wants to buy you clothes

Blaire
Everybody likes Pretty Woman, there was nothing else to watch.

George
Keep telling yourself that

Blaire
Who's idea of happiness involves getting swept off my feet. That's a kidnapping

George
You keep pretending and you might miss out on your fairy tale

Blaire
Give a fuck! Disney lied

George
You're not special, you want a happy ever after just like any other girl. This is why no one understands women...

Blaire
Oh poor men, such beautiful complex and majestic creatures forced to exist in a world amongst us feeble vessels.

George
I don't have a problem with how women are

Blaire
Feeble vessels?

George
I just think you're complicated

Blaire
You can't be that dumb. I refuse to believe that I'm fighting for equality to be with the likes of you

George
You have it easy. You marry rich or you sell pus..

Blaire
I have aspirations actually. I don't intend to waste my life

George
Aspirations for what? Stressing yourself out for no reason. As a man//

Blaire
Don't give me that rubbish about bringing home the bacon. When men have squandered the economy senseless to the point that one income households are living in poverty

George
And you think filing papers and answering phones will push us into the next tax bracket

Blaire
Fuck you

George
Fuck you!

Blaire
Fuck! Two minutes with you and I've lowered my standards

George
You're right women shouldn't swear

Blaire looks at George in disgust

It's vulgar and unladylike.

Blaire
I don't need the title thank you

Halle comes down the stairs in fancy heels ready to go

SCENE SIX

George and Halle walk back after their date night

Halle
Thanks for tonight

George
Any time

Halle
I quite like the place actually

George
Feel like the waitress fancied me

Halle
You think everyone fancies you, woman at the desk at the pharmacy, the post lady

George
She put an x on my prescription

Halle
To sign here!

They both laugh

Halle
This is nice we don't get to do this
Set us back £80

George
You don't have to worry about that

Halle
I know I don't have to but I'd like to be on top of savings

George
I got us covered

Halle
Since being with you, I think I've heard that 96 times

George
You just worry about what colour our curtains will be

Halle chuckles unsure if she should be offended or not

I'll budget how much it'll be to reconstruct Blaire's room

Halle
Yeah she'd like that

George
Would she? I reckon she'd make up every excuse not to move out

Halle
Move out?

George
Yeah or where else is she going to live?

Halle
I just thought...
I thought all three of us would

George bursts into a fit of laughter

George
Now I know you're joking

Halle
I just don't feel comfortable with that idea

George
What the idea of living with the person you love

Halle
I've never been without Blaire, quite frankly I don't see how she'd cope

George
It's not up to you to baby sit her

Halle
I don't. I just think she's going through some things

George
Yeah dicks

Halle
God George that's my best friend

George
You need to stop defending her. She hardly talks about you in the best light

Halle
Ok so well fall out, but we make up again

George
You're miles ahead of her Halle

Halle
I'm not telling her she needs to move out

George
Not straight away but she has about a year to get her shit together
Don't know how much more I can take of the chick

Halle
Even if she moves out she'll still be in my life

George
Yeah your life
Look this was a good night don't let her ruin it.

Halle
She hasn't ruined anything it's you

George
Come on, you're mad at me because I want my girlfriend to myself?

Halle
Can we go home.

SCENE SEVEN

Narrator
Day Seven of rehabilitation when wounds don't heal they leave ugly scars

Nurse
What do you fear the most?

Blaire
It's between Wasps and Psychopaths. I wouldn't want to be stung by either one

Nurse
I think you misunderstand me

Blaire
I choose not to live my life in fear

Nurse
I'll let you in on one of mine. I fear not being able to help you. If I couldn't it'll probably keep me up at night

Blaire
I know the feeling

Nurse
Not being able to help

Blaire
No, being up all night

Narrator
Faces begin to flash before my eyes and my heart begins to beat and I remember what it's like to be free briefly before I'm captured and encaged. I have this reoccurring dream

Nurse
Tell me about it

Blaire
I wake up every night at 4:23 am and I think for approximately twelve minutes and then I drift back to sleep

Nurse
Twelve minutes?

Blaire
I've timed it

Nurse
Thinking about

Blaire
What my life would be like if...

Blaire stops and jolts forward, then swallows the speech

Nurse
What your life would be like if...

Blaire
If you're scared of helping people you shouldn't be a nurse, surely

Nurse
It depends if you let fear cripple you or you make a habit of overcoming

SCENE EIGHT

Blaire
Come in!

George walks in

Blaire
Oh it's you again. Stuffs by the dryer

George
Thanks

I thought you'd have more to say

Blaire
Nah

George
Oh come on.

Blaire
I think maybe you should do your washing yourself. Like a big boy

George
There it is

George takes a seat next to Blaire

Halle doesn't like how starchy I get my collars

Blaire
Ask her how it's done

George
What does it matter if she want's to do it?

Blaire
I doubt she wants to do it

George
She's a good girl, she doesn't mind

Blaire
There's no such thing

George
You can't turn a whore into a housewife so I guess there is

Blaire
The fact that you're so bold as to determine whether or not a women is good or bad tells me that you've got this God complex.
Well let me break it down to you. At no point in my life would I ever strive to hit someone's standard of how I should be. Especially from men

George
I'd beg to differ

Blaire
Of course you would

George
Again contradiction. Your entire political stance circulates around how men perceive women. The content of all your conversations have been men. You compare yourself to every man ever. I think it's your first thought of the day. You revolve around us

Blaire
Don't flatter yourself

George
Please forgive me but I'm only going off of what you give me

Blaire
Well let me do the same. You've got a large ego to compensate for you inability to fathom simple ideologies. You're spineless and you're nothing without someone to trample on

George
You got all that from what I give off?
I wonder how you're so good at reading when you're forever alone

Blaire
Society have made up this idea that a woman is incomplete by herself. When really God didn't want man to be alone.

George
I don't buy it

Blaire
I'm not selling
No but isn't that your whole argument, that men were made first so they are the greatest?
George and Blaire both smirk

George
I don't buy this 'Independent, I don't need a man coat' you're trying to wrap yourself in

Blaire
You don't have to

George
Women have been fighting for how many years now for equality? Don't you think if it was written in the stars, it would have happened by now?

Blaire
I think this patriarchal society would collapse if women had more of a say and men are scared of that
George
I think you need a stiff drink and a stiff dick.
George grabs Blaire by the next sexually as he delivers these lines

SCENE NINE

Narrator
Day Nine of Rehabilitation. Do I have victim on my forehead? Do I some how invite prey?
Faces begin to flash before my eyes and my heart begins to beat and I remember what it's like to be free briefly before I'm captured and encaged. I have this reoccurring dream

Nurse
This is a little impromptu but I'm here to listen

Blaire
I was twelve and he was fifteen, he should have known better. But men are never held accountable for what they do.

Nurse
Your first boyfriend

Blaire
Who was tall for a year ten, and had slits in his eyebrows, back in the day when it was in
He was fifteen and I was twelve
He made me feel special

Nurse
Special?

Blaire
And then he took it away. Like they always do, they give and then take away. Like they're gods but they're not

Nurse
Blaire tell me what happened

Narrator
Faces begin to flash before my eyes and my heart begins to beat and I remember what it's like to be free briefly before I'm captured and encaged. I have this reoccurring dream

Blaire
I often ask myself the same question. Because it wasn't just him

Blaire
For the last time pick up your laundry and go.

George
You're hysterical

Blaire
Hysterical, Crazy, Psycho- Blaming words. Men need someone to blame in order to perpetuate this idea that they are divine. I'm not going to be the punching bag

George
I'm just saying you get your knickers in a twist about things you can't change

Blaire
You're the wall blocking the promise land. I want men like you to crash down like the walls of Jericho. You don't deserve to be where you are. You are making zero impact. Zero

George
What exactly is your legacy Blaire? Berating women for being too prude?

Blaire
I've never, name one person I've done that to

George
Halle

Blaire
Halle?

George
Called her a doormat, a male sympathiser, a disgrace to the female race?

Blaire
Yeah I said that but I'm passionate about the cause

George
Fuck the cause. You're a bitch. I really thought you were going to deny that

Blaire
Why am I a bitch? Because I have a voice, I have an opinion.

George
You're all bark and no bite. Don't take it out on my girlfriend because she's feminine
Blaire
Feminine? You mean weak.

George
I mean what I said

Blaire
You said that in order for a woman to be feminine she needs to be meek, timid and have her boyfriend fight her corner

George
You really do make this shit up

Blaire
That's what you said! That's what I heard! You just had a different way of saying it.

George
Calm down

Blaire
Don't tell me to calm down. Don't tell me to shut up or back off. I'm allowed a moment.
George waits awkwardly whilst Blaire is emotional

Beat

George
You're so messed up, what happened to you?

Narrator
Faces begin to flash before my eyes and my heart begins to beat and I remember what it's like to be free briefly before I'm captured and encaged. I have this reoccurring dream

George
I wonder if you would have a boyfriend by now if you weren't always trying to cut off their balls and wear it for yourself

Blaire
I've had boyfriends

George
Is that what you're calling them

Blaire
I've had boyfriends George

George
Ok so why not try ones that actually stick around.

Blaire
How about you get a girlfriend that has a mind of her own and not a ventriloquist dummy

Halle walks in having heard Blaire

Blaire
Halle I didn't mean

Halle
No it's okay, you think I'm stupid

George
You see what I mean

Halle
I have backed you up on numerous occasions when people have said you mistreat me. I've championed you at every turn

Blaire
He got on my nerves and I had to say something to get to him

Halle
I'm not falling for it anymore

Blaire
I just wish you would stand up for yourself a bit more. You're weak

Halle
-

Beat

Halle
Hold on, you don't get to call me weak, I don't jump from man to man just because I've noticed something in a guy that's a minor inconvenience to me. You do that! That's weak. Not me and my relationship.

Blaire
You think the freedom of choice is weak. There were women who burnt their bras Halle

Halle
For a voice, for an identity. Not for penis musical chairs!

Blaire
Well use your voice. Don't let him take over your dreams, the Halle I knew would have hated this. You're trapped

Halle
The Blaire I knew was a friend and she had so much love inside her. It's like looking at the cold dead carcass of the friend I once had

Blaire
You think because you have the fancy job, and the boyfriend and the sensible haircut that you're one step away from the white picket fence but you're not. You're as low down and dirty as the company you keep. You're filthy just like me

Halle
I think it's time you moved out

Black out for slightly longer than usual

SCENE TEN

Light comes back on. Blaire and Narrator are standing opposite each other mirroring each others sequence of movements before Blaire crashes to the ground on her knees

Narrator
Day twelve of rehabilitation, hurt people hurt other people. So what am I doing here if I can't make a positive effect?
Faces begin to flash before my eyes and my heart begins to beat and I remember what it's like to be free briefly before I'm captured and encaged. I have this reoccurring dream
Its 4:23am I'm tired of waking up

Blaire
Still on her knees, she raises her head to the sky
This punishment seems a little too severe. I wonder if he wakes up at night. I wonder if he thinks about what I'm doing with my life, if my face haunts him. I wonder if he can't forget I wonder if he can't forget

Narrator
4;35am and I drift back to sleep. Twelve minutes. I couldn't sleep for twelve minutes

Nurse
Have you been writing things down?

Blaire
Yes

Nurse
Good, and what have you noticed?

Blaire
That I fear him

Nurse
Your first boyfriend

Blaire
He was tall for a year ten, he had dark brown eyes and slits in his eyebrows. Back when it was in. He was fifteen and I was twelve. It took him twelve minutes to rape me. I fear him

Nurse
You're very brave. Thank you for sharing

Blaire
I'm not brave. He's still walking free.

Narrator
Faces begin to flash before my eyes and my heart begins to beat and I remember what it's like to be free briefly before I'm captured and encaged. I have this reoccurring dream

Nurse
When people are abused, they tend to build an unhealthy relationship with sex and relationships

Blaire
Which is why I scored 86% on that test

Nurse
Which is why you're sat here with me
Unhealthy relationships do not only stem from misuse or abuse. It can sometimes not be our fault. Like in your case. It wasn't your fault.

Blaire
I've read hundreds of cases and none of them sound like mine. I feel complicate. Like I egged it on

Nurse
It's not just you, many people misunderstand what consent is, they misunderstand rape in itself. They believe it's someone jumping out of a bush or tying you up against your will. On the contrary 6 out of 10 victims say they knew their attacker

Blaire
So Nympho or not.com were wrong?

Nurse
Blaire who else knows?

Blaire
Him

SCENE ELEVEN

Blaire is waiting on a bench for Halle, Halle is running late.

Halle
I'm here

Blaire
Thanks for coming

Halle
If you're going to beg about coming back to the flat

Blaire
No it's not that

Halle
What is it Blaire, I got an hour for lunch

Blaire
Nice weather

Halle
Yeah sure

Blaire
I wanted to apologise for my behaviour. It was wrong
I have no right to dictate what kind of woman you are or should be

Halle
But?

Blaire
But what?

Halle
You always have a but Blaire

Blaire
I came to apologise that is all. It's just

Halle
There it is

Blaire
No, hear me out please

Halle
Okay

Blaire
I've missed you, I've missed us. I feel like we used to be fun and do shit together

Pause

Halle
Remember that shit date you went out with what's his name again? He was really blonde but really tan

Halle/Blaire
Victor!

They both laugh

Halle
He took you to dinner and

Blaire
He couldn't understand that sexism was not a made up concept

Halle
Then you spat at him

Blaire
It just came out. I promise you it wasn't planned

Halle
I had to run up there and get you, told the manager you were a bit off and dragged you out

They both continue to laugh

Halle
I've been saving your arse for twenty years now, what would you do without me?

Blaire's mood drops

Blaire
Get into a ton of trouble. I'm sorry I haven't had your back, the way you've had mine

Halle
It's fine

Blaire
No it's not fine Halle.

Halle
Why not I'm telling you that it is

Blaire
Because you deserve better, you deserve me to be a better friend and to treat you the way you treat me. At least. In fact you deserve a better boyfriend

Halle
Oh no don't start

Blaire
You know I'd tell you the truth. If you would stop lying to yourself you'd see that he's not what you want

Halle
Oh and you know

Blaire
I have a rough Idea, I've known you for twenty years, George isn't it.

Halle
I think about it sometimes, but I'm willing to fight for it

Blaire
It's a losing battle

Halle
Hey! Nobodies got a crystal ball into the future

Blaire
No I don't but I know you can't see him in yours. What are you scared of?

Halle
I'm not scared

Blaire
Then leave him. Start again. I'll be with you every step of the way

Halle laughs

Blaire
I mean it

Halle
I know, but I'm not scared, but I appreciate your help but this time you've got it wrong

Blaire
If you can just think about it

Halle
I don't want to hear anymore. My lunch break is over. Your boxes are still at the flat

SCENE TWELVE

Narrator
Day Thirteen of rehabilitation. Not everyone is going to counseling with you. Faces begin to flash before my eyes and my heart begins to beat and I remember what it's like to be free briefly before I'm captured and encaged. I have this reoccurring dream

Nurse
How are you feeling today?
Blaire
Good a little lighter than normal

Nurse
Good thing?

Blaire
I guess we've made some progress

Nurse
You've made progress

Pussy Liberty by Valerie Isaiah Sadoh

Blaire
I once tried to do the splits in year six, because Jessica Renner could do it. She was like world class gymnastics for under elevens
During play time she would gather the boys and do her splits and other moves

So I came into school one day with a leotard under my uniform and told my whole class that I'd just come back from a competition in Crystal Palace and when they asked for proof I'd lift up my shirt and show the leotard. All the boys believed me.

After all a little healthy competition was good for you, Jessica told me that. After a week of coming to school with my leotard, Jessica got annoyed with all the attention I was getting and challenged me to a gymnastics off and I accepted. Knowing full well that I had no idea what I was doing.

We got outside to the playground and I dropped down into a forced split and tore my inner thigh muscle. Was off school for weeks, everybody knew I lied. Embarrassing.
It's funny what's embarrassing when you're a kid

Nurse
I can imagine that of you Blaire

Blaire
I didn't learn my lesson though.

Narrator
Faces begin to flash before my eyes and my heart begins to beat and I remember what it's like to be free briefly before I'm captured and encaged. I have this reoccurring dream

Blaire
When I got to secondary school Sophie Rylan was the first to lose her virginity in year seven she had an older boyfriend in year nine. She got all the attention. So one day I was late to school and everyone was looking for me.
I came in about third period and my friends were shocked. I could have told them that I skived off at the back of the leisure centre. In stead I said I had an older boyfriend in year ten.

Everybody wanted to know about him where we met, I started getting all the attention, so after a week of talking to about my imaginary year ten boyfriend Sophie asked me what sex felt like. I didn't know, I hadn't done it

I couldn't answer, embarrassed. So after school all the guys and girls ganged up around me and Sophie and she asked me who my older boyfriend was, what was his name. The space fell silent and I thought the gig was up, but then he stepped forward.
He was tall for a year ten, he had dark brown eyes and slits in his eyebrows. Back when it was in. He was fifteen and I was twelve. He stepped forward to say he was my boyfriend. And I went with it. He became my boyfriend.

Nurse
It still doesn't make it your fault

Blaire
But I contributed?
My mum used to say that your words breathe life, I just didn't know she meant literally

Nurse
No Blaire, he abused his power

Blaire
Why couldn't I see that? Nothing in that moment rang bad idea, he's evil. Stop the lie, nothing

Beat

Nurse
If you see fire, you avoid it. If you see fireworks, you're enticed. Sometimes danger is wrapped up in

Blaire
Dark brown eyes, with slits in his eyebrows. Back when that was in

Blaire smiles to herself, not out of happiness but realization

Blaire
Feel like I can't get the blood off my hands. It's like paint

SCENE THIRTEEN

Scene changes into the flat where George is measuring the space between walls and the doorway, Halle enters with pots of paint.

Halle
So I've got three types of greens

George
Not the white that we discussed

Halle
I know but you said I had the final say, I quite like the outdoors

George
Since when?

Halle
Since I saw the green in the Dulux section

George
Who's house have you been in that you've seen green walls?

Halle
We can be the first

George
You've lost the plot

Halle
So what brush do I start painting with?

George
None we're using rollers

Halle
Ok so where is it?

George
We're nowhere near painting

Halle
Just give me the roller and I'll give it a bash

George
You've got to strip the walls first

Halle
I'm pretty sure I've just painted over in the past

George
Unless you want this place to look like a shithole. I suggest you strip the wall

Halle
Ok fine what do I use to strip the wall?

George
You know what I'll do it

Halle
Just tell me what to use and I'll do it

George
No, go sit down or make tea for both of us. Yeah that'll be helpful

Halle proceeds to walk to the kitchen which is the direction of off- stage

Halle
Actually no.

George
What?

Halle
No. I don't feel like making tea. I'm quite capable of stripping a wall

George
It's a mans job Hal, I'll just do it after this, what's gotten into you?

Halle
Some sense

George
What?

Halle
Nothing!

George
You've been acting strange

Halle
I'm just slightly uncomfortable

George
It's a big change I know, but it'll be worth it

Halle
I can't catch my breath

George
Don't be overwhelmed, we can take it step by step

Halle
I seem to be suffocating

Halle grips the collar of her shirt in a fanning motion

George
Have you opened the paint, it's the fumes

Halle
Got this banging headache

George
Walk away from the paint

Halle
Seeing double
Halle stubbles around almost about to faint

George
This is why I said let me do it, you've probably bought toxic ones

Halle
It's NOT the damn paint George it's us

George
Oh

Halle
I can't breathe because of us

Beat

George
You don't want to move in

Halle
It's not that

George
Renovating your place was your idea, I said you could move into mine

Halle
I made those plans when I was nineteen

George
Ok so

Halle
So, I was talking out of my arse

George
Why bullshit me?

Halle
I wasn't intentionally. I was saying what I thought you wanted to hear

George
Fine. Return that then
George points at the pots of paint Halle walked in with

Halle
Honestly no hard feelings

George
I wasted six years of my life, so you throwing no hard feelings at the end, doesn't make it anymore easier

Halle
I don't want to end things babe

George
I can't keep going at this snail pace. It's killing me

Halle
You're quite dramatic

Halle tries to lighten the mood with a smirk and slight nudge

George
When I met you I told you what I wanted

Halle
Yes. You did

George
Now all of a sudden you're suffocating

Halle
It wasn't all of a sudden, actually it was quite gradually and steady

George
I don't know where this is coming from

Halle
I apologise for that. But like you said you told me and I followed. I thought that that was what my role was. To follow. But lately I just feel like a robot

Halle begins to make robot like movements

George
I get it

Halle
No but you don't and you never will. Because there is no pressure on you

George
Well you'd be wrong. There is pressure and I feel it everyday, thank you

Halle
You don't know what it is like to constantly open Facebook and see the girls you went to school with advertise their engagement rings.
To be questioned by family about the progress of our relationship status and not a single question about me and my well being.
It's always about us and I've lost myself keeping up with the Jones'
Oh and if I open Facebook one more time and see an ultrasound I may lock myself in a dark room for a week.

George I have never failed, ever. Being with you seemed like the correct box to tick. I wanted so bad to pass the exam of life that I didn't think about where that leaves me. I simply suppressed my emotions.

George
You don't think I get the same

Halle
No one asked you if you're ready for kids

George
Ok, they don't. But I'm under pressure too. I'm working more that forty hours a week and I still needed four months to pay off my bike. And I needed a fucking bike because travelling to work was burning a hole in my pocket.
I'm doing a Tour de France to work everyday to save £9.60 because that £9.60 is the difference between having a flat to get back to.
I want to do more for you.
Even if I saved up three months salary for an engagement ring, I'd have to get it from Goldsmiths.

Halle
But you don't get it. I don't want to get married. I don't want children. It was all a lie, George

George
So what are we doing?

Halle
Not making this lie legal

SCENE FOURTEEN

Blaire is still talking to nurse

Blaire
I have this reoccurring dream.

Narrator
Faces begin to flash before my eyes and my heart begins to beat and I remember what it's like to be free briefly before I'm captured and encaged. I have this reoccurring dream

Blaire
I keep having it, it's like I'm a bird have you ever walked down City lane and seen those Pigeons with one leg. Yeah I'm one of those and I'm flying soaring through the sky spreading my wigs. I feel free, invincible. I'm speeding, can't hear my surroundings because of how fast I'm going. Oh God I love it.

But you can't fly forever, you need to eat. So as I'm descending to the ground with my eye on the prize. I suddenly remember. I've only got one leg. I've only got one leg.

Nurse
And you think that means

Blaire
Nobody can give those pigeons on City Lane their leg back

Nurse
Right

Blaire
But they still have a life to live, they just got to adjust their technique

Nurse
So you're the legless pigeon?

Blaire
Yeah! I'm the legless pigeon.

Nurse
You can still have your happy ending Blaire. You don't have to settle for less. You're not a legless pigeon, You're Blaire.
You can still wear white, you can still live your own romantic comedy, you can still have kids. What he did to you has no bearing on the type of man you're allowed to have. He doesn't determine the outcome of your life. He is does not give. He cannot take away

Blaire
He

Nurse
Your first boyfriend

Blaire
He was tall for a year ten, he had dark brown eyes and slits in his eyebrows. Back when it was in.

He has no control?

Nurse
He has no control. It's time for you to live for you

SCENE FIFTEEN

Blaire has finally decided to pick up her boxes from her and Halle's old Flat, as she looks through boxes and sees old photos of her and Halle she tears up. Then the door opens. George enters wanting to return his key

Blaire
I can never have a moment without you

George
Hiding the fact he has a key to return
I guess great minds think a like

Blaire
So

George
Just here to pick up

Blaire
I didn't see any washing for you

George
No not here for laundry

Blaire
Learnt to do it yourself?

George
I have indeed

Blaire
I'm proud

George
So I'll just be getting... are those pictures of you and Halle

Blaire
Yeah, still haven't spoken to her. Just wanted to be in an out

George
Oh, I know your intentions
They both laugh

Blaire
Seriously she doesn't know I'm here

George
Doubt she knows I'm here either

Blaire
Yeah but she won't mind

George realizes Blaire doesn't know their current situation

George
What do you think about green walls?

Blaire
For where? A shed.

George
No for a house

Blaire
A greenhouse?

George
No an indoor house

Blaire
I know I disagree with you for habit but green walls is a little much

George
I thought so

Blaire
Shouldn't you be...

George
Returning a key

Blaire
No!

George
Yeah, it's a wrap

Blaire
You and Halle

George
Yeah

Blaire
Oh piss off, I can't be nice to you when you've gone and broken my best friends heart. Get out!

George
I doubt she's heartbroken

Blaire
You're her life

George
Life of lies. She called it off

Blaire
Yes.
No. Why?

George
She don't want kids

Blaire
Right now it's a bit early, she's got like loads of her twenties left and you've got a solid three years of it left. It's a bit soon

George
Ever.

The room falls silent, George becomes visibly upset. Blaire awkwardly comforts him

Blaire
George, she never told me

George
Turns out she's this mastermind liar

Blaire
No, she not

George
Then she said no hard feelings like, like that was meant to heal something

Blaire
She probably changed her mind along the way and didn't know how to say it. It might change back

George
Not with kids

Blaire
I can't lie I'm pleasantly surprised. I didn't think men minded.
Having kids or not

George
I just want to do it right.

Blaire
Maybe she'll change her mind

George
I don't want her too

Blaire
She's having a little wobble

George
It's more than a wobble, she looked relieved

Blaire
That she got it off her chest

George
Like she broke out of this

Blaire
Reoccurring dream.

George
Well I'm going to leave my keys

Blaire
I have reoccurring dreams

Narrator
Faces begin to flash before my eyes and my heart begins to beat and I remember what it's like to be free briefly before I'm captured and encaged. I have this reoccurring dream

Blaire
You know I thought you were a bad guy, but. I mean this is the first time I've seen this side of you

George
This is the first time you've listened to me

Blaire
I admit, I rarely listen, but men barely have anything substantial to say

George looks at Blaire

Not all but most, ok a fair few

George
Bye, Blaire

Blaire
No, stay, well at least help me carry this box back up to the shelf

George helps Blaire

Blaire
Who's mum were you talking about?

George
When?

Blaire
You said, it's hard having a mum that regretted

George
Hypothetical

Blaire
Haha, for a second I thought you knew something about my mum and I

George
No, I was just thinking

Blaire
I haven't called her in ages, guess I have a reason to now. Need somewhere to live

George
I bet she'd love that

Blaire
I guess you've got to call your mum too

George
Not really

Blaire
You've already told her about Halle

George
Nothing to tell her, she never knew

Blaire
What! she never knew!

George
She's got her own things going on

Blaire
Makes sense

George
How?

Blaire
Why you're so angry at us?

George
I'm not angry at anyone

Blaire
You are angry at women. Yes you are
Because of your mum

George
So what got you so messed up?
Dad issues

Blaire
Have no dad issues

George
So you're theory fails

Blaire
Nah you got mummy issues. You've got to let them go. You can't live life like a legless pigeon. I heard that once

George
Crazy

Blaire
I think it's crazy that I didn't figure this out sooner haha. You've got mummy issues damn!

George
Every time, I think there's a human being behind those eyes. Turns out you're just Nazi Feminist through and through

Blaire
That's got nothing to do with!

George
You always have an agenda

Blaire
What's wrong with fighting for what you believe in?

George
You've gotten lost in the fight
I was trying to talk to you

Blaire
Me? You hate me

George
Well you've known me for five years, you're a friend by default. And a shit one at that.

I've lost everything.

Blaire
You haven't lost everything, you don't know what it's like to lose everything

George
You would know

Blaire
Mr high roller. You want for nothing in this world. You call the shots

George
I don't call anything.

Blaire
Macho Macho George. When you walk in the whole room we all stand to attention!

Blaire salutes as she stands to attention

George
Nonsense

Blaire
You're words are heavily weighted

George
Bullshit! I have no jurisdiction!
With anyone

Blaire
Have you no eyes to see?
I fight constantly to be at your level

George
Well then you're on the wrong battlefield.

Blaire
You've got so much power in this world and you're wasting it, because mummy said you weren't enough

George
You don't know anything about my mum

Blaire
You've just been talking about her for the last half hour

George
Look don't mention her

Blaire
What is she upset with you?
Don't like the flat your living in
The watch you're wearing doesn't have enough diamonds for mummy!
Did she hurt you?
Did mummy hurt you?

George
Yeah. She did

Blaire
Oh George, I was joking I didn't

George
Think

Blaire
I was winding you up, you always do it to me
George
I'll take that as an apology

Blaire
Parents aren't super heroes, sometimes they get it wrong

George
She got it so wrong
Practically raised myself because she was so engulfed with getting things wrong
Like fear controlled her life.

She wouldn't come to any of my parents evenings, in case I was behind on homework and she didn't know why.
Wouldn't cheer me on at games, in case we lost and she didn't have the words.
She wrote me letters and slipped them under the door. Some subjects were just a little bit too confrontational for her. I mean how pathetic?

She stayed with my stepdad for nine years, said she hated every minute of it but didn't know how to say it.
And then I go and get the same damn person, who can't speak up until it's too late.

Pathetic!
All my life I just wanted mum to stand up for herself, or at least for me

Blaire
I don't think she's a bad person

George
I don't know, maybe she was sick
Spent everyday till now proving to her that I was stronger than that. I could do it better.
Be a better person, parent eventually.
Maybe it wasn't her fault

Narrator
Faces begin to flash before my eyes and my heart begins to beat and I remember what it's like to be free briefly before I'm captured and encaged. I have this reoccurring dream

SCENE SIXTEEN

Narrator
Day Fourteen of rehabilitation, you're not the only one. Everyone has pain.

Blaire
I told you about George didn't I?

Nurse
Your roommate's boyfriend

Blaire
My best friends boyfriend, ex. Turns out he's a dick because of mum issues. I didn't think of that.

Beat

Nurse
You think about Sophie Rylan ever?

Blaire
Nope!

Nurse
Why not?

Blaire
I just don't

Nurse
When you said she asked you what sex felt like, you made it sound like she was attacking you

Blaire
Yeah!

Nurse
What if she was asking for help?

Blaire's face drops from the stern bitch face

What if she was asking for reassurance, confirmation?
That what happened to her, happened to you.

Blaire
No.

Nurse
Sometimes we forget that other people have their own issues

Blaire
No.

Nurse
It might not have changed what happened, but it could have been her too

Blaire
But she always seemed so ok.
Normal

Free

Narrator
Faces begin to flash before my eyes and my heart begins to beat and I remember what it's like to be free briefly before I'm captured and encaged. I have this reoccurring dream

Nurse
Sophie might have been faking

Blaire
Why would she need to?

Nurse
Same reason you did

Blaire
Embarrassed. Didn't want to feel used or weak. She was a nice girl Sophie. Strong. Maybe she thought that no matter what situation she got herself into she could get out of. Or maybe she trusted too easily, thought that if she was strong enough life wouldn't hurt her.
And then felt like a fool, when she couldn't say no when she needed to. That in that very moment when she needed a voice her voice failed her. Maybe she froze, when all she wanted to do was get out! Get up and leave! Why didn't she move? Why!
Maybe she expected more from men. These perfect creatures who know it all and can do no wrong. Maybe she expected them to know what a 'no' looked like. Or felt like.

Nurse
Her?

Blaire
Him
My first boyfriend. Tall for a year ten, with dark brown eyes and slits in his eyebrows back when it was in. Was her same demon, was her same reoccurring dream

But she was so cool, popular I didn't think. We all ignored the signs, ignored her pain. No one looked her in the eye and said We know.

Blaire stands up and shouts

We know. Sophie I know and I believe you. I believe you. I believe you.

Narrator
Day Sixteen of rehabilitation. A milestone.
`I'm part of a larger story. Not a story of the victims. But the survivors.

Me and Blaire.

Blaire
Me and Sophie.

Blaire and Narrator hold hands and black out.

End

www.ingramcontent.com/pod-product-compliance
Lightning Source LLC
Chambersburg PA
CBHW071037080526
44587CB00015B/2653